BJ
REV

10/97

10.30

Paul

3-5

Cornerstones of Freedom

Paul Revere

Gail Sakurai

CHILDREN'S PRESS®
A Division of Grolier Publishing
New York • London • Hong Kong • Sydney
Danbury, Connecticut

CALUMET CITY PUBLIC LIBRARY

Library of Congress Cataloging-in-Publication Data

Sakurai, Gail.
    Paul Revere / Gail Sakurai
        p. cm.—(Cornerstones of freedom)
    Includes index.
    ISBN 0-516-20463-7 (lib.bdg.)   0-516-26230-0 (pbk.)
    1. Revere, Paul, 1735–1818—Juvenile literature. 2. Statesmen—
Massachusetts—Biography—Juvenile Literature. 3. Massachusetts—
Biography—Juvenile Literature. 4. Massachusetts—History—
Revolution, 1775–1783—Juvenile literature. I. Title. II. Series.
F69.43S25 1997
974.4'03'092—dc21
[B]   97-717
                                                                CIP
                                                                 AC

©1997 Children's Press®, a Division of Grolier Publishing Co., Inc.
All rights reserved. Published simultaneously in Canada.
Printed in the United States of America.
1 2 3 4 5 6 7 8 9 0 R 06 05 04 03 02 01 00 99 98 97

On the night of Tuesday, April 18, 1775, the road to Lexington lay empty and silent in the moonlight. Families slept behind closed doors and shuttered windows. Then, from a distance came the *clippety-clop* of a galloping horse. The sound grew louder, and a moment

Paul Revere rides by moonlight to the town of Lexington.

later a horse and rider raced into sight. They pulled up in front of a farmhouse, and the man banged on the door. "The regulars are out!" he shouted. A light flickered, then burned steadily in an upstairs room. A farmer threw open the shutters and stuck his head out the window. But the rider was already charging along the road to the next house, where he repeated his warning that the British army was on the march. The messenger's name was Paul Revere.

Paul Revere was born on December 31, 1734, in Boston, the largest city in the British colony of Massachusetts. He was the oldest son of a French immigrant named Apollos de Rivoire. The English-speaking people of Boston had trouble pronouncing the French name, so Apollos changed it to "Revere."

Revere designed and crafted this teapot.

Young Paul attended school until he was thirteen, when he began working in his father's silversmith shop. He was talented and a quick learner. Soon he was making silver shoe buckles, spoons, and teapots. When Paul was nineteen, his father died. It became Paul's duty to run the silversmith shop and provide for his mother and seven brothers and sisters.

But Paul Revere also had a duty to serve his country. Like many other young

men in Britain's American colonies, Paul Revere
volunteered to fight against the French during
the French and Indian War. When he was
twenty-one, Revere served for one year as a
second lieutenant in the Massachusetts army.
Along with other volunteers from Massachusetts,
he participated in a failed attempt to capture a
French fort in upstate New York.

*French and
English forces
fought bitterly
during the French
and Indian War.*

Rachel Revere

After his year of military duty, Paul Revere returned to Boston. He fell in love with Sarah Orne, and they were married in August 1757. The young couple soon started a family and eventually had eight children. Sadly, Sarah died in May 1773. But Revere was not lonely for long. He soon met Rachel Walker, and the two were married in September 1773. Paul had eight more children with Rachel. Of Revere's sixteen children, five died at a young age.

Paul Revere continued to work in his silversmith shop. By this time, he was widely recognized as one of the best silversmiths in Boston. But times were hard and few people could afford expensive items made of silver. To help support his growing family, Revere learned to make false teeth. He also taught himself engraving and printing. He was quick and clever and enjoyed learning new skills.

Revere engraved this view of Boston.

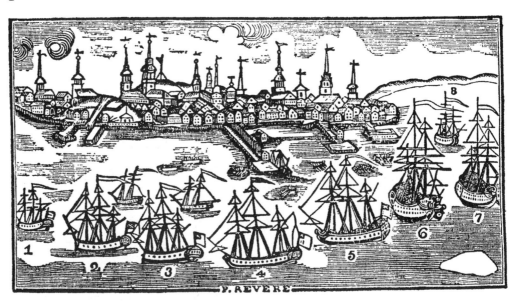

Soon he would be using his new abilities for political purposes.

Although Great Britain had won the French and Indian War, the war had been long and expensive, and Britain was deeply in debt. The British Parliament decided to raise funds by placing taxes on a variety of goods that were imported into the American colonies. Many Americans resented these British taxes. They reasoned that since the colonies had no representatives in the British Parliament, the Parliament had no right to tax the colonies.

Colonists had to pay taxes in the form of stamps.

Colonists gather to protest British taxes.

Paul Revere was an important member of the Sons of Liberty, a secret society of colonists who organized public protests against British taxes. The Sons of Liberty also urged the colonists to boycott all British goods. When American protests against the taxes became violent, Great Britain sent soldiers to Boston to restore order. The citizens of Boston hated having the red-coated British "regulars" in their town. Anger between the colonists and the redcoats reached a crisis on March 5, 1770.

On that date, an unruly mob of Boston residents began throwing rocks at a small group of redcoats. The frightened soldiers fired their

At a meeting, the Sons of Liberty discuss strategies to fight the taxes.

guns into the crowd, killing five people. The incident became known as the "Boston Massacre." American rebels used the event as an excuse to stir up opposition to British rule. Paul Revere engraved and printed a political drawing of the Boston Massacre. The print was not an accurate picture of what happened. It showed evil-looking redcoats firing on peaceful and innocent citizens. Revere's engraving helped turn public opinion against the British.

Revere's rendition of the Boston Massacre fueled anti-British sentiment throughout the colonies.

Colonists dump tea into Boston Harbor.

In response to colonial protest, Parliament canceled all the colonial taxes except the tax on tea. The Sons of Liberty, however, were still not satisfied. They argued that Parliament had no right to collect even the small tea tax. American "patriots" who refused to buy British tea drank coffee instead, or they used tea smuggled in from the Netherlands.

Then, in December 1773, the British East India Company sent three ships loaded with tea to Boston Harbor. The Sons of Liberty would not let the ships' captains unload their cargo. The rebels tried to persuade the British colonial governor to send the tea ships back to England, but the governor refused. The Sons of Liberty decided to convince Great Britain that the colonies were serious about fighting the tea tax.

On the night of December 16, around 150 men and boys disguised themselves as American Indians. They boarded the three tea ships, the *Eleanor,* the *Beaver,* and the *Dartmouth,* which were docked at Griffin's Wharf in Boston. Paul Revere had helped plan the "tea party," and he was among one of the three boarding parties. The "Indians" threw 342 chests of tea into Boston Harbor as a protest against the tea tax. The next day, Revere rode on horseback to New York and Philadelphia to spread the news of the Boston Tea Party to patriots in the other colonies.

To enforce the authority of the Crown, British soldiers enter Boston.

The Boston Tea Party made the British Parliament very angry. Six months later, on June 1, 1774, Great Britain closed the port of Boston as punishment for the Tea Party. Britain sent four thousand soldiers and a fleet of warships to keep Boston Harbor closed until the town paid for the ruined tea.

At that time, the city of Boston was located on a small peninsula in Boston Harbor. Only a narrow strip of land, called Boston Neck, connected the city with the mainland. Boston received most of its food and supplies by ship. When the British closed the port, they cut off the usual supply route. The British intended to starve the citizens of Boston into submission.

Once more Paul Revere rode as a messenger for the Sons of Liberty. He carried the news of the harbor closing to patriots in New York and

In the 1770s, the city of Boston was almost completely surrounded by water. The only way to get in or out of the city by land was over Boston Neck. Paul Revere would begin his famous ride on April 18, 1775, by rowing north across the Charles River to Charlestown.

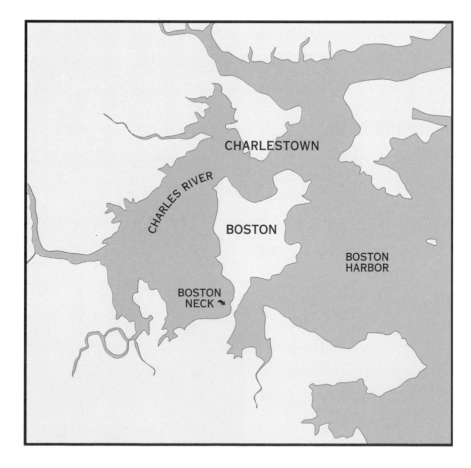

Philadelphia. As the story spread, other colonies responded to Boston's need. They would not let the city starve. Supplies began to pour into Boston by the land route across the Neck. Sheep and cattle arrived from the nearby countryside. Rye, flour, and codfish came from other Massachusetts towns. South Carolina sent rice, Maryland sent wheat, and Pennsylvania sent money. The thirteen American colonies united and supported the people of Boston in their struggle against the British.

After the closing of Boston Harbor, clashes between British soldiers and Boston citizens became more common.

In response to the British soldiers, militia units began drilling and stockpiling weapons and ammunition.

The increased tension between Britain and the American colonies made war seem likely. Every colonial town had a militia, a group of local men who were trained to fight and defend their homes. Now the militias began drilling and preparing to fight the British. Militia leaders also started storing weapons, ammunition, gunpowder, and other supplies in secret hiding places.

By the spring of 1775, rumors had been flying for weeks that the British were planning to take action against the rebels. Paul Revere helped organize a group of about thirty artisans and craftsmen to spy on the British. Revere's spies met in great secrecy at the Green Dragon tavern in Boston. At every meeting, each man had to swear on the Bible that he would never reveal anything that was said. The spies patrolled the streets of Boston in pairs, keeping watch on the movements of the British soldiers.

A sign hung outside the Green Dragon tavern

On Saturday, April 15, Revere's spies learned that the British governor of Massachusetts had ordered his troops to prepare for a mission. Dr. Joseph Warren, a leader of the Boston patriots, suspected that the British would march to the town of Concord to capture the weapons and ammunition the militias had hidden there.

Dr. Joseph Warren

Two important rebel leaders, Samuel Adams and John Hancock, were staying in Lexington, just a few miles from Concord. Dr. Warren feared that the British would arrest Adams and Hancock and send them to London to stand trial for treason. If convicted, they would hang. Warren decided to send Paul Revere to Lexington to warn Adams and Hancock. Revere had become the rebels' most trusted and dependable messenger. Boston patriots nicknamed him "Bold Revere."

John Hancock

Early on the morning of Sunday, April 16, Paul Revere rowed across the Charles River to Charlestown. He borrowed a horse from Colonel William Conant, head of the Charlestown militia. To avoid arousing suspicion, Revere rode slowly. He pretended to be taking a leisurely Sunday ride in the country. Revere met with Adams and Hancock in Lexington and warned them of the British plans. Then he continued on to Concord and advised the leader of the Concord militia to move the military supplies to safer hiding places.

Samuel Adams

3 1613 00243 5256

CALUMET CITY PUBLIC LIBRARY

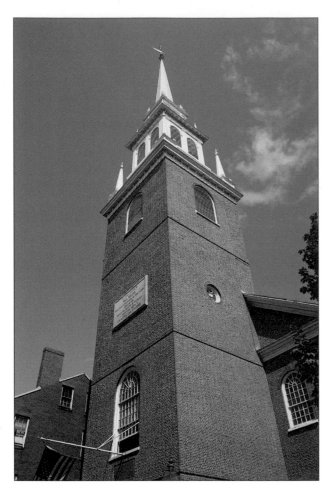

The Old North Church today

On his way back to Boston, Revere returned the borrowed horse to Colonel Conant. He promised to alert Conant when the British marched. The two patriots arranged a signal, in case a messenger could not get out of Boston. Christ Church, also called the Old North Church, was Boston's highest building. Rebels across the river in Charlestown could easily see a light in the church's steeple.

"If the British went out by water we would shew two lanthorns in the North Church Steeple, and if by land, one, as a signal," wrote Revere. "For we were apprehensive it would be difficult to cross the Charles River, or git over Boston neck." Patriots in Charlestown would keep watch for the signal—one lantern meant a land crossing and two lanterns meant the British were crossing by water.

Paul Revere returned home and waited for word of the British movement. Around nine o'clock on the evening of Tuesday, April 18, a messenger called him to Dr. Warren's house. Revere's spies had learned that seven hundred

British troops were gathering at that moment on Boston Common, a large open field next to the Charles River. The soldiers were preparing to take longboats across the river to Cambridge. From Cambridge, they would march to Lexington and Concord.

Dr. Warren had already sent one messenger, a young man named William Dawes, to Lexington by the long land route. But Warren worried that Dawes would not be able to get past the British sentries at the Neck. Paul Revere wrote, "Dr. Warren . . . begged that I would immediately set out for Lexington, where Messrs. Hancock and Adams were, and acquaint them of the movement."

The British soldiers rowed from Boston to Cambridge.

Bold Revere agreed to attempt the shorter but more dangerous water route across the Charles River. On his way home to pick up his coat and riding boots, he stopped to see Robert Newman, who was the caretaker at Christ Church and a loyal Son of Liberty. Revere told Newman to light two lanterns in the church steeple. Revere wrote, "I then went Home, took my Boots and Surtout, and went to the North part of the Town, Where I had kept a Boat."

"Two friends rowed me across the Charles River, a little to the eastward where the Somerset Man of War lay," Revere said. The HMS *Somerset*, a British warship, was anchored in the middle of the river to prevent anyone from crossing. Paul Revere knew he would have to be very careful and quiet or the British would catch him. The slightest noise could alert the armed guards aboard the *Somerset*. Revere and his friends borrowed a flannel petticoat from a neighbor. They tore up the petticoat and wrapped the strips

In order to row across the Charles River safely, Revere had to be very careful of the British guards on the HMS Somerset.

of cloth around the oars to keep them from creaking in the oarlocks.

Paul Revere crossed the Charles River safely, in spite of the bright moon that was rising. Patriots in Charlestown who had seen the signal lights met Revere and loaned him a horse. They warned him that British patrols had been riding earlier that evening on the road to Lexington. The redcoats would surely be on the lookout for rebel messengers.

Revere immediately set off for Lexington. Just outside Charlestown, as he was crossing a desolate area of marshes and clay pits, he spotted two British officers on patrol.

"The moon shone bright," Revere wrote. "I saw two Officers on Horseback, standing under the shade of a Tree, in a narrow part of the roade. I was near enough to see their Holsters & cockades. One of them started his horse towards me . . . I turned my horse about, and rid upon a full gallop."

A clay pond lay directly ahead. Tall marsh grass hid its steep sides. Revere swerved at the last moment, avoiding the pond's slippery banks, but the British horse slid and became stuck in the clay pit. Revere said: "I got clear of him . . . and after that, I alarmed almost every House, till I got to Lexington." Before long, everyone along the road between Charlestown and Lexington knew that the British army was marching that night.

Across the Massachusetts countryside, colonists heard the alarm.

Paul Revere galloped into Lexington and went straight to the home of the Reverend Jonas Clark, where Hancock and Adams were staying. Revere warned the two rebel leaders to leave Lexington at once. Half an hour later, William Dawes rode up. He had passed the guards at the Neck by pretending to be a drunken farmer.

After a short rest and some food and drink, Revere and Dawes decided to ride to Concord and warn the patriots there. Just outside Lexington, a young Concord physician, Dr. Samuel Prescott, joined them. Prescott had been in Lexington visiting a lady friend and was on his way home.

After escaping from the British officers, Revere warned local farmers that the British soldiers were coming.

The house where Hancock and Adams stayed

He offered to help the two Boston men spread the alarm.

About halfway to Concord, Prescott and Dawes stopped at a farmhouse to give the alarm, while Revere rode ahead. Suddenly, two British officers on horseback surprised him. "Come up!" he shouted to his companions. "There are two of them!"

As Prescott and Dawes approached Revere, four more British officers rode up. Revere, Dawes, and Prescott were forced off the road and into a meadow. Realizing that they were about to be captured, Revere told his companions to flee in different directions. Prescott jumped his horse over a low stone wall and got away. He was the only rider to reach Concord that night. Dawes managed to escape, but lost his horse. Revere galloped toward a small wood, but just as he reached it, six more redcoats rushed out and grabbed his horse's bridle. Bold Revere was captured.

By this time, patriots were firing warning shots and ringing bells to alert the whole countryside. The British officers were worried about getting back to their army without running into armed militiamen. They could travel more easily without a prisoner. They finally decided to let Revere go, but they kept his horse.

Paul Revere made his way back to Lexington on foot. He arrived at four in the morning and found Adams and Hancock just leaving. The two patriot leaders invited Revere to ride in the carriage with them and John Lowell, Hancock's personal secretary. A mile down the road, Lowell remembered that he had left a trunk full of Hancock's important papers at Buckman Tavern, where he had been staying. Those papers contained secret information, such as names of rebel leaders and spies, that should not fall into British hands. Revere and Lowell decided to walk back to Lexington and hide the trunk at the Reverend Clark's house.

John Lowell left an important trunk in Buckman Tavern.

Revere and Lowell reached Buckman Tavern near the Lexington Green just as the sun rose. Young Willie Diamond was beating the call to arms on his drum, and the Lexington militia was assembling. About seventy militiamen formed two lines on the triangular Green. From an upstairs window in the tavern, Revere "saw the British very near, upon a full March."

Revere and Lowell carried the trunk across the Green. At that moment, a shot rang out. Revere turned his head toward the noise, but a shrub blocked his view. No one knows for certain which side fired that first shot. By the time Revere and Lowell had safely stored the trunk at the Clark house, the shooting was over.

This map shows Paul Revere's ride on April 18–19, 1775.

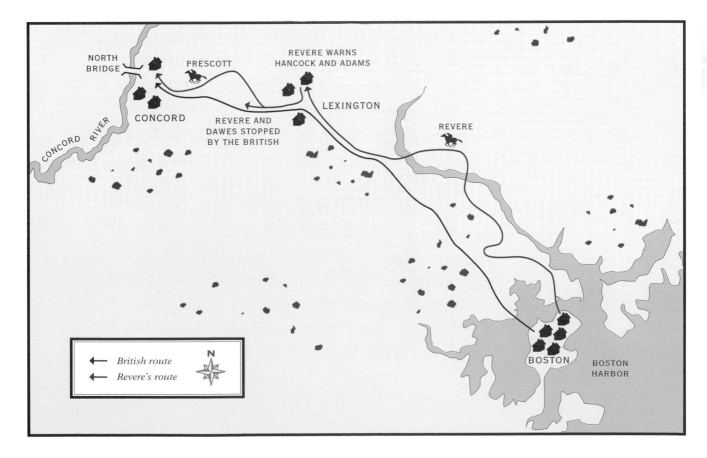

NORTH BRIDGE

PRESCOTT

REVERE WARNS HANCOCK AND ADAMS

CONCORD

CONCORD RIVER

REVERE AND DAWES STOPPED BY THE BRITISH

LEXINGTON

REVERE

BOSTON

BOSTON HARBOR

← *British route*
← *Revere's route*

N

At Concord, the British soldiers were driven back by the colonial militia.

Eight patriots lay dead on Lexington Green, and ten more were wounded. The British gave a traditional victory cheer and marched on to Concord, where another brief battle took place later in the morning. The American Revolution began that day with the battles of Lexington and Concord.

During the war, Paul Revere used his many talents for the benefit of the patriot cause. Rebel leaders frequently asked Revere to mount his horse and carry important messages for them. Since he was already a skilled engraver and printer, he also engraved and printed the first money for the new Massachusetts government.

Revere printed currency for the Massachusetts government.

When the Massachusetts army ran short of gunpowder, they asked Paul Revere to set up a powder mill and produce the needed gunpowder. Revere knew nothing about making gunpowder, but as always, he was an eager and quick learner. He visited powder mills and studied diagrams of powder-making equipment. Then, he supervised the establishment of the new powder mill and the production of its gunpowder.

When the army desperately needed more cannons, they once again turned to Paul Revere. He found a master cannon maker and studied his techniques. Then, Revere arranged for cannons to be produced and shipped to Boston.

In addition, Paul Revere served as lieutenant colonel in the Massachusetts army for three years. He was one of the officers in charge of defending the city of Boston. In 1779, Revere and his troops were ordered to take part in a large military expedition against the British forces in Maine. The Maine mission did not go well for the Americans. The army blamed the navy for the failure, and in turn, the navy accused the army's officers of disobedience and cowardice. Revere was upset by the accusations and insisted on a court-martial to clear his name. Finally, in 1782, Revere received his trial and was found innocent by the court.

Paul Revere & Son,
At their BELL and CANNON FOUNDERY, at the
North Part of BOSTON,
CAST BELLS, of all fizes; every kind
of Brafs ORDNANCE, and every kind of
Compofition Work, for SHIPS, &c. at the fhorteft notice;
Manufacture COPPER into SHEETS, BOLTS,
SPIKES, NAILS, RIVETS, DOVETAILS, &c. from Mal-
leable Copper.
They always keep, by them, every kind of
Copper faftening for Ships. They have now on
hand, a number of Church and Ship Bells, of dif-
ferent fizes; a large quantity of Sheathing Copper,
from 16 up to 30 ounce; Bolts, Spikes, Nails, &c
of all fizes, which they warrant equal to Englifh
manufacture.
Cafh and the higheft price given for old Copper and Brafs.   march 20

Paul Revere never lost his eagerness for learning new crafts. After the American Revolution ended in 1783, he taught himself to cast bells. His first bell weighed over 900 pounds (409 kilograms) and was cast in 1792 for his own church in Boston. Some people thought that the tone of this first Revere bell was rather harsh and shrill. After that, Revere insisted that purchasers approve a bell's tone before

Revere advertised his bell manufacturing in local papers (above). The USS Constitution *(right)*

the sale would be considered final. If buyers were dissatisfied, Revere agreed to refund their money. Over the years, he cast more than four hundred bells for churches and public buildings all over the United States. His largest bell weighed 2,437 pounds (1,105 kilograms).

Paul Revere continued to master new skills. He learned how to roll copper into sheets. In 1800, he set up the first successful American factory to produce sheets of rolled copper. Some of Revere's copper sheets were used to protect the bottoms of American warships, such as the famous USS *Constitution,* known as "Old Ironsides." He also rolled copper sheets for the dome of the new State House in Boston and for the roofs of many other public buildings.

Paul Revere became a successful and wealthy businessman. He continued to be active in politics his entire life. Revere spent his later years happily surrounded by his children, his grand-children, and his dear wife, Rachel, who died in 1815. Paul Revere himself died on May 10, 1818, at the age of eighty-three.

By the time he grew old, Paul Revere was a prominent citizen in Boston.

Today, nearly two hundred years later, there are still many reminders of Paul Revere's place in American history. Visitors can tour Paul Revere's house in Boston's North End. The Paul Revere Memorial Association restored the house and opened it as a museum in 1908. Other museums contain such historic items as John Hancock's trunk, a signal lantern from the Old North Church steeple, and many fine pieces of Revere-made silver. The copper company that Paul Revere founded still exists today and is a leading producer of rolled copper and copper products.

The Paul Revere House today

But Paul Revere is best known for his part in the events leading up to the American Revolution. Many books, stories, and poems have been written about Bold Revere and his actions on the night of April 18, 1775. Perhaps the most famous retelling is Henry Wadsworth Longfellow's long narrative poem, *Paul Revere's Ride,* first published in 1863. The Boston silversmith, soldier, businessman, and patriot will always be best remembered for "the midnight ride of Paul Revere."

The opening lines to Longfellow's Paul Revere's Ride

LISTEN my children, and you shall hear

Of the midnight ride of Paul Revere,

On the eighteenth of April, in Seventy-five;

Hardly a man is now alive

Who remembers that famous day and year.

GLOSSARY

ammunition – bullets or balls fired from a gun or cannon

boycott – to refuse to use or buy certain goods as a protest

cast – to shape liquid metal by pouring it into a mold

The Boston Tea Party was part of a colonial boycott of British tea.

cockade – knot of ribbon worn on a hat as a badge

colony – territory that is far away from the country that governs it

court-martial – trial by a military court

engrave – to carve, cut, or etch into a surface used for printing

immigrant – person who leaves one country to live permanently in another

Parliament – group of people responsible for making the laws in Great Britain

patriot – person who loves, supports, and defends his or her country

peninsula – body of land surrounded on three sides by water

The Sons of Liberty were patriots.

rebel – person who fights against the established authority

sentry – guard

surtout – wool overcoat

treason – crime of betraying one's country

TIMELINE

1734 Paul Revere is born

French and Indian War ends **1763**

Boston Massacre **1770**

Boston Tea Party **1773**

Boston Harbor is closed **1774**

1775

1776 Declaration of Independence is signed

1783 American Revolution ends

April 18: Paul Revere's midnight ride

April 19: Battles of Lexington and Concord

1818 Paul Revere dies

1863 Longfellow's poem, *Paul Revere's Ride,* is published

1908 Paul Revere house opens as a museum

DEDICATION
For my mother

INDEX (*Boldface* page numbers indicate illustrations.)

Adams, Samuel, 15, **15,** 17, 20, 22
American Revolution, 23–25
Boston, Massachusetts, 4, 6, **6,** 11, 12–13, **12,** 14, 25, 26, 28
Boston Massacre, 8–9, 10
Boston Tea Party, 10–11, **10**
Concord, Massachusetts, 15, 17, 20, 21
    battle of, 24
Dawes, William, 17, 20–21
French and Indian War, 5, **5,** 7
Hancock, John, 15, **15,** 17, 20, 22, 28

Lexington, Massachusetts, 3, 15, 17, 19, 20, 22
    battle of, 23–24
Longfellow, Henry Wadsworth, 29
Lowell, John, 22–23
Paul Revere's Ride (Longfellow), 29, **29**
Prescott, Samuel, 20–21
Revere, Paul, 27
    in American Revolution, 23–25
    birth of, 4
    and Boston Tea Party, 10–11

    as copper sheet manufacturer, 27–28
    death of, 27
    as engraver and printer, 6–7, **6,** 9, **9,** 24–25, **25**
    in the French and Indian War, 5
    and midnight ride, 3, **3,** 18–23, **18, 20, 23**
    as silversmith, 4, **4,** 6, 28
    and the Sons of Liberty, 8, 10, 12, 18
Sons of Liberty, 8, **8,** 10, 12, 18
Warren, Joseph, 15, **15,** 16, 17

PHOTO CREDITS

Photographs ©: Corbis-Bettmann: 4, 15 middle; Culver Pictures: 14 top; James P. Rowan: 16, 21, 28, 31 bottom; The Metropolitan Museum of Art, Arthur Hoppock Hearn Fund, 1950: 1 (painting by Grant Wood); Courtesy Museum of Fine Arts, Boston, Gift of Joseph W., William B., and Edward H.R. Revere: 2; 31 top right; New England Stock Photo: cover (Thomas Mitchell), 22 (John Wells); North Wind Picture Archives: 5, 6 top, 7, 8, 9, 11, 14 bottom, 15, 18, 20, 24, 25, 26 bottom, 27, 30 bottom, 31 top left; Stock Montage, Inc.: 3, 6 bottom, 10, 13, 17, 26 top; 30 top.

Maps by TJS Design.

ABOUT THE AUTHOR
Gail Sakurai is a children's author who specializes in retelling folk tales and writing nonfiction for young readers. She is a full member of the Society of Children's Book Writers and Illustrators. Other books she has written include *Jamestown Colony, The Liberty Bell, Mae Jemison,* and *Stephen Hawking.*

   Ms. Sakurai lives in Cincinnati, Ohio, with her husband and two sons. When she is not researching or writing, she enjoys traveling with her family and visiting America's historical sites.